THOUGHTS
OF ONE
WOMAN, AS
SHE READS
HER OWN MIND

THOUGHTS OF A ONE WOMAN AS SHE READS HER OWN MIND

BY

TONI L. STREETER

About the Book

Thoughts Of One Woman, As She Reads Her Own Mind is a collection of poetry that was written to touch a part of every woman. All of us feel and live things in our lives that we think we deal with alone, not realizing that there are others that feel the same.

I hope that this book will help others see that there is someone else out there that knows how they feel and understands.

Please enjoy.

TABLE OF CONTENTS

PASSION

LET ME INTODUCE MYSELF

There once was a woman, we'll call her passion. Why passion, you may ask? The name passion touches all that she is. Her life, her love, her mind, and her heart. Passion was created out of love, somewhere long ago in the quiet of another world, shielded from the pain of what existed in the outside world. In her world, she was like others, she knew of the sweet prince and the lovely princess, and the fairy tales that made life always have happy endings.

As passion grew, tiny parts of the cold outside world made it's way into her sheltered life. She learned of cold hearts. She learned of pain. She also learned she could survive in this cold outside world by finding the pleasure in putting herself in a state of euphoria with the help of alcohol and sometimes drugs. Sometimes even the warmth of a man's arms to shield her, make her forget the hurt. She thought this was the meaning of happiness. Poor passion, she was wrong. So much more was to be learned.

The following poems are a part of passion's heart, mind,

and soul, how she has been touched, and what she has learned in the process. I invite you to read passion's mind, she feels that she holds within her a thought, a feeling, or an emotion that may also touch another woman. A woman in the same time and place in her life as passion, that feels she is no one. That she has nothing to offer but her heart and knows that with offering her heart, there is the high risk of pain and damage. Sometimes, damage she feels cannot be repaired.

Please keep in mind that passion has learned, there is real love that exists in a world she thought so cold. There is repair for the heart that has been broken, sometimes over and over again. Her name, passion, reveals her darkness inside, searching for pleasure to mask her pain. But also it tells of her hunger for learning and growing beyond her pain, beyond her broken heart. Maybe, what you read will open your eyes to the same.

SHE, HER TINY BITS AND PIECES

She is warm, yet cold as ice
She is darkness, with an inner light
She is seen by many eyes
Yet she is hidden, protected
Under heavy lock, she holds her secrets
And very few are allowed a key
She is like a dancing cobra
Beautiful, hypnotic
But underneath the beauty, she is poison
She is like the cat, soft, sensual
And like the cat
She has a sharpness
It makes you afraid to touch her
She can soar like an eagle
But stays grounded, for she fears falling
She has tears
She has smiles
She has an inner strength
She has an inner fear
She loves to be held

She loves to hold

She plays the role of the giver

As well as the taker

But when she takes

She wants your soul

She is easy to satisfy

But is never satisfied

She looks in the mirror

She sees many faces

Joy

Pain

Love

Rage

Passion

Aggression

So many faces in the mirror she sees

And all the faces in the mirror she sees

She admits to herself, they are me........

Passion's Pain

Passion has seen pain in her life, not unlike many other women. But Passion closed her mind to the things in her life that caused the pain, trying hard to pretend it didn't exist. The following poems came to life when Passion opened her eyes...................

THE THEFT OF INNOCENCE

When she was very young
You were family
Cousins, but close
You played together
Like brother and sister
You, much older
More of a role model
Always patient with little kids
Always teasing the little girls

When she began her teen years
You saw her differently
You saw a woman
She was still a child
You felt lust
She still felt like climbing trees
You still teased her

But it was different than before
Now when you teased
You always had to touch her
She was still a child
Not knowing the touch was a sign
A sign of something wrong

Innocent pokes to her tummy
She was ticklish, she laughed
From behind, a soft squeeze on the neck
Or pulling the pig tails she still wore
She saw nothing wrong
She was still a child

In the darkness you came to her
This time the touch was different
This time she did not laugh
She did not feel teased
She felt dirty
She felt shame
She felt pain

You left her there

Left her in the darkness

Her thoughts confused

She slipped back into her sleep

Hoping she could make it a bad dream

It would be gone in the morning

You would be gone in the morning

It wasn't a dream

She couldn't make it go away

You invaded her young life

Changing it forever

When you left her you took something

Something that could not be replaced

Something she would miss throughout her life

You took what was left of her inner child

You took her innocence

MOMMA CRIES

She knows it was her fault
The pain in momma's eyes
Out of all of the children
She was the one
The one who caused the tears
Making momma cry

When the family turned their backs
She was the cause
When momma was sad and alone
She was the cause
She felt her momma's tears
When she looked into her eyes

She tried to avoid it
She learned to do drugs
Just one more hit,
Maybe it will go away
She learned to drink
Just one more shot

Maybe it will go away

Nothing was strong enough
The alcohol, the drugs
She still saw momma's eyes
She still felt momma's pain

She sometimes looked elsewhere
Trying to find comfort
She tried the arms of a man
But, just like drugs and alcohol
The effect was temporary
The thoughts of momma always came back

She grew and functioned as normal
Or, at least as society felt was normal
But, not a day went by without the thoughts
The thoughts of the damage she had caused
Too late to change it
She could never go back

Someday maybe she will realize
Momma cried for her

Not because of her
As she was feeling momma's pain
Momma felt her pain
Momma cried out of love
Love for a daughter
A daughter in pain

IS IT REAL?

Is it real when he says

I love you

Soft spoken words

The look in his eyes shows her

It is real

But, can she define love

Does she know how it feels

The promise of true love

True love promised for all time

Is it real

We say till death do us part

But, for how long

It is now so easy to walk away

So easy to begin again

I love you

Holds so many promises

Promises made when we say, I do

Promises meant to be broken

Didn't we mean them at that moment

This is real

A cold and lonely heart

Fearing the thought of trusting again

Or making promise after promise

Hoping to get it right someday

I love you

Such beauty in those words

But, how long does it last

Until the youth and beauty is no more

Until the sexual pleasure fades

This is real

Finding the one true love

Knowing that he is part of you

Making love until you feel you are one

One mind, one heart, one soul

I love you

Yes it does have meaning

Yes it can be forever

But, have we lost touch

Has there been so much pain

We have forgotten

What is real

THREE PHASES OF LOVE

He wants her
He has to have her
The woman of his dreams
His touch is soft
She gives him all of herself
Her mind, body, and soul
He has her, now what
The fantasy is over
Now, he owns her heart
He will never let go
She feels alone
No longer special to him
She has her duties to perform
No room for mistakes
She has been given everything
She must in return give everything
She is always cold
No one to hold her
She is always sad
No one to make her smile
It wasn't supposed to be this way
She doesn't sleep much anymore

Because the dreams she once had

Are now nightmares.....

NIGHT SCREAMS

As she sleeps, she feels him
She knows he is coming
The man from the shadows
He only comes in the darkness
Only while she is sleeping
He knows when she is weak

She fears him, no where to hide
She tries to make herself free
Something holds her
Her mind screams for help
Her heart feels pain
The hands, she sees the hands
His face is dark, angry
Those hands want to hurt her

She runs for freedom
For her there is none
She stops, hiding like a child
He has something of hers

Something that keeps her close
He knows how to find her
He knows how to bring her out
Closer to him, keeping her there
The hands grab her
Clutching her throat

Feeling her last breath
The last thing she sees
Is the angry shadow, smiling
She awakens, sweaty, shaking
Who is he, why can't she see his face
He seems so familiar to her
What does he have that was hers
How does he keep her so close
Her heart, he holds her heart

Her heart she gave to him
She gave this gift willingly
She gave it freely
She gave this gift of her heart
A gift she thought he would cherish
Hold it close

Keep it safe
Keep it warm

With the gift of her heart
He has done these things
She has felt cherished
She has felt close
She has felt both safe and warm

But while she sleeps
Her heart fights with her mind
A long constant painful battle
What her heart calls love
Her mind calls possession
Her mind recalls the pain for her
Her mind screams in the night
Showing her heart the reality
Her heart tries to hide
Wanting to make believe love is blind
And wanting to feel secure

But as she sleeps
Her mind makes her heart see

Makes her look at her past

Look at the pain she endured

Makes her remember every blow

Makes her see in the mirror

Looking into her past

Seeing the bruises

Seeing the tears

Her heart blocked her mind

So long ago

Her heart wants only to see the good

Never the bad, but inside her mind

She does remember, it is so clear

It was like a training period

Early in their life together

She sees and remembers all now

She was taught not to raise her voice

Punishment was pain

She was taught not to walk away in anger

Punishment was pain

She was taught not to fight back

Punishment was pain

She was taught not to disrespect

Punishment was pain

And when she cried
She was left alone
He would not hold her
Nor would he look at her
And never did he utter those words
All she ever wanted to hear
He never said..............
I never should have touched you in anger,
I love you and I am sorry
All she ever heard............
It was your fault, you made me do it

She learned over the years to behave
No more pain
She learned not to anger him to that level
No more pain
Now she holds anger deep, don't fight back
No more pain
Her heart feels happy
Her mind feels imprisoned
Her heart holding the keys

But her heart is weak in the night

And her minds screams

She sleeps

And her mind screams

She dreams

And her mind screams

Now she has fear

Fear of sleep

Fear of the man in the shadows

Fear of her mind's screams

DESCENDING

She walked on the edge
She had no fear
Suddenly she lets go
Plunging into the deep end
For a time she floats
She feels no fear
Then she realizes
There is nothing to hold
No way to get out
She is floating
There is no escape
She struggles
It takes her deeper
Her mind cries for help
But her voice does not speak
Over her head now
She fights, wanting air
There is none
She is going deeper
But, she stops struggling

No longer caring

She sees herself drowning

She only waits for the end

She opens her mouth

Hoping it will end sooner

But the end is slow

The last breaths long

Her mind grows numb

Her heart grows cold

She is aware

But at the same time

She sleeps

Slow and painful is death

When you find yourself

Drowning in your own life

THE SILENT FRIEND

She lies awake, night after night
She doesn't hear the voice......
All seems quiet, no one to turn to
She feels alone

As she spends her days privately thinking
She doesn't hear the soft whispers......
Telling her it will all work out
She feels all alone

She felt there was no one
No one she could call best friend
She cries inside, hurt and lonely
She feels alone

She has gone though many changes
She has felt much happiness
She has felt much pain, but....
She realizes she wasn't alone

As a woman she hears the voice
She is learning to listen
Hearing the soft whispers
She has a very dear friend

Her friend has been there all her life
Staying close but quiet
She has closed her mind for so long
She thought her best friend was no more

Now she sees this dear friend
Learning to love her once again
The friend helps her realize
She is never alone

She has someone to love
Someone who is with her forever
She finally re-discovered
How to be a friend to herself

SHE, HER DARK PASSION

She has no heart

She has no love

She has but one single driving force

Her pure dark passion

This makes her sleep

This makes her eat

This quenches her thirst

But for now she waits

Her hunger not fed

Her thirst not quenched

She finds it hard to sleep

She is so restless

So weak

She is pure dark passion

And she is slowly fading away......

Passion's inner thoughts

Sometimes we watch the world around us and just wonder about some of what we see. The following poems are reflections of these thoughts..........

WHAT IS THE A TRUE MEANING OF LOVE

She looks at her life
She has an open heart
She tries to keep an open mind
She has loved deeply
She has loved long
Why does she feel pain
Why does she accept that pain
Why has she been confused

She knows love is tenderness
She knows love is sharing
She feels those feelings
She enjoys the thought of being loved
Sharing her heart with another
But sometimes love hurts
It leaves wounds that refuse to heal
She has accepted these wounds, as part of love

But is this the way it's suppose to be
Is love supposed to hurt

What does it mean

In her life love has always had a price

Happiness in exchange for the pain

This is what she has learned

This is how she lives

Now she questions her life

But why......

Has she not been deserving of true love

Does she not understand the true meaning

Is it her fault, choosing to accept both love and pain

Or is it a learned behavior

Is life possible without pain

This she knows

The answer is simple.....no

Is there balance

In life there is happiness

She has felt this

In life there is pain

She has felt this also

Should the happiness overcome the pain

She thinks........

The answer is simple.....yes

But where does she find true happiness
This is where confusion begins
This is where her mind asked the question
What is the true meaning of love
She takes a long look at herself
Looking inside, trying to find answers
What choices does she make for her future
She cries, not knowing

She is split, torn in half
Fighting an inner battle with herself
Half wanting to continue on
Half wanting to let go of this life
Needing to start over, try and do it right
She blames herself for her unhappiness
She blames herself for her pain
The choices she made brought her to this moment

What does she do
How does she live from this moment on
Is she too late
Can she find the truth
The true meaning of love.....

COMFORT

When we are babies

And we get upset

We get our pacifier

It is comfort

When we are toddlers

It is taken away

They say we are too old now

When the toddler needs calming

They sometimes suck their thumb

It is comfort

When we are preschoolers

It is stopped

They say we will ruin our teeth

As school children and pre-teens

We twist our hair

We bite our nails

It is a comfort

But we don't want to look like kids

So we learn to stop ourselves
We grow to break our own bad habits

So young, so tense
What do we do now
No pacifier
No thumb
No nail biting
We are all grown up
What do we do

Now, as adults
Bad day at work
A drink of alcohol after hours
Yes, that makes us feel better
That is the grown up thing to do
Then we find we need two
Then three, more and more
Alcohol, our comfort zone
And now, we feel bad
How did we get here
How do we break this habit by ourselves

Hard day with the kids

Just a cup of coffee

It will help, just a little

Caffeine will give me energy

We can keep up with the kids now

We go for one cup

Next thing we know

We are drinking a whole pot

Caffeine, our comfort zone

How did we get here

How do we break this habit by ourselves

There is still one other

But it is ok we don't do it like some

Just sometimes

That's what we tell ourselves

We light one with that drink

After a hard day at work

Nicotine, our comfort zone

How did we get here

How do we break this habit by ourselves

We have to have one with our coffee

They seem to go so well together

Then we find ourselves needing them

We have to have them

We get angry if someone tries to take them away

We know the danger

We know who this killer is

Nicotine, our comfort zone

How did we get here

How do we break this habit by ourselves

We make excuses

But it is comfort

It is soothing

Oh, I don't smoke that many

And we have many more

But we know it has us

And we know what it does to us

How did we get here

How do we break this habit by ourselves

Nicotine, our comfort zone

How did we get here

How do we break this habit by ourselves

Alcohol, caffeine, nicotine
They are ok, we are grown ups
Have we made a choice
Do we want to shorten our lives
Is everything around us that bad
For some, they search for secrets
Secrets to long life
They are blessed
They are not where we are
They knew how to break their own habits
All by themselves

For some, all they search for
Is their cigarettes , need a smoke
Or, they search for that next drink
Caffeine, alcohol, doesn't matter
As long as they feel better for the moment
As long as they have their comfort
How did we get here
How do we break these habits by ourselves

What we should really be asking ourselves
Is why did we ever come here

And why don't we choose to break these habits

We are all grown up

And we made these choices

A WOMAN'S FEARS

There was a time, so long ago
A woman felt free
She slept with windows open
Enjoying the cool spring breeze
There was a time when a woman felt free
Going out alone was a natural thing
She enjoyed walks in the park
Alone with just her thoughts
There was a time when a woman felt free
Her children played in their yards happily
A woman was in her kitchen cooking
Not on constant watch

But now it is different
A woman fears going out alone
She fears the risk of not making it home
Walks alone in the park, are no longer safe
She fears the thought of assault or rape
When her children play
She drops everything to watch

For she fears the stranger's approach
Why is it now she must live in fear

Somehow, somewhere, something was lost
Woman was made for man by god
A woman was made to be loved
A woman was made to be cherished
A woman was made to aid in mans strength
A woman was made to stand by man's side
To be united for life, be fruitful, and multiply
But somehow, somewhere, something was lost
For now, for many women
Their biggest fear
Is man.......

MAN AND LION, WHO IS THE BEAST?

You watch the lion
He walks on four legs
Here we are different

The female gives birth in the wild
We give birth in a sanitized environment
Here we are different

The female lion shows she is the source of strength
Providing food, she is the hunter
Knowing without her, the family dies
Here we are different

The female protects her young from predators
Keeping them close, until they can care for themselves
Tender care given with every touch
Here we find no difference

Sometimes the female destroys her young
Or sits by as the male harms her young ones

The lioness will die protecting her cubs
Here we are different

The beast sometimes has to fight for their food
The strongest overpowering the weak
Leaving the weak to die alone
Here we find no difference

The weak are abandoned or killed
Left for the scavengers to pick away at whatever is left
We watch, as if the death surrounding us is normal
Here we find no difference

When male and female lion join for life
The lion is there until death do them part
We say the words, but often walk away
Here we are different

The family of the lion is a true bond
Protecting each other and sticking together
Here we find it easier to turn our backs, or breaking the
bond
Here we are different

The lion lives his life knowing no god
Man lives his life denying god exists
Man and lion mark their territory, proudly showing what is
his
Here we find no difference

Man boasts of being above the lion
He studies the lion as a lower form of life
Man places himself above all animals
Look closer, are we really??????

Passion's Pleasure

Passion is a very sensual lady that learned after the age of thirty to appreciate her erotic side. She understands this side of herself now, and takes pride in the fact that sexuality in a woman is something that when nurtured, can be just as strong as the loving side of being a woman. Passion has found this to have no limit. The following contains parts of Passion's sexuality, her fantasies, and her pleasures................

THE DREAM

As she woke slowly, smiling, she knew

He had come to her

Her skin was still warm, moist with sweat

She knew it was the afterglow

She squirmed and stretched

She could still see him

She could still smell his scent on her body

Her lips still trembled from his goodbye

Oh yes, fully awake, now she sees clearly

Then came the tears

As she wrapped her arms around herself

She held on tight

Fully awake, in the darkness alone

She realizes

It was only a dream

THE FANTASY

Lying in her bed
Her body still warm from her bath
She calls him
The phone rings once, twice
She holds her breath, hoping he answers
He says hello
And her heart for one long second stops
She tells him she misses him
He feels the same
They chat, she smiles
But inside she wants more
While he speaks softly to her
She feels herself being drawn to him
The words he speaks
Take her mind to another realm
The sound of his voice
Soothes and comforts her
On her journey to this other realm
She feels the rhythm of his breathing
It awakens her sexual senses

She closes her eyes and slips very quietly

Into the realm where only he and she exist

She wants him

He knows her so well

She is in some ways afraid

She knows that even though he does not see her

He has the power to reach out and touch her very soul

She hungers for him

He holds her, caressing her mind with his soft words

She can't resist him

She can no longer contain herself

Slowly she rocks her body

Moving to the sound of his every breath

She can almost hear his heart beat

She touches herself

Teasing her womanhood with her fingertips

She is so warm, so wet

Wanting his touch so badly

Her body aches for him

He holds her

He comforts her

She hears his voice and feels at ease

She allows herself to touch her wetness

Letting her fingers go deep, deep inside

She touches and plays with her special place

And she is so eager to share that special place with him

She is so hot

Yet she trembles

She is drowning

She gasps for every breath

He holds her

He gives her strength

She releases her caged animal

She squirms, clenching her teeth

Her breath is heavy

In her mind she is in his arms

She explodes with a passion so unfamiliar

It takes her breath away

She is ashamed for one moment

Then she realizes, yes, he is with her

And she feels so good

Slowly, satisfied, she smiles

Then drifts quietly into his waiting arms

Knowing he always waits for her in her dreams

For so long, she was slipping away
She felt she had died inside
Now, into her mind, body, and soul
He breathes new life........
As she waits (the fire within)

There is a small fire that burns within
Small embers glowing majestically
As she waits for her lover to come for her
She knows that his love will feed those embers
The embers become a flame
A roaring fire fed by their passion and desire for each other
At last, together they create a bonfire that is so hot
The heat of their passion melts the two hearts into one
Resulting in one single, powerful, beautiful, climaxing moment
And that moment, is pure ecstasy......

PASSION'S WEB

She is like the black widow

And she is pure beauty

Her beauty, though haunting

Is like a magnet

Drawing you closer

You touch her

You hold her

You are caught

You can't seem to release her

But you don't care

In her embrace

Is where you want to be

All that you were, is no more

Every breath you take is her

All your eyes can see is her

You smell her scent

Your mouth knows her taste

You wake at night hungry for her

She loves you

She holds and caresses you

She spins a loving web

It binds your heart

And you smile at her

Drifting deeper into her web

It's what you hunger for

It is her passion

And it feeds your hunger

Her passion is yours forever

But for you, forever is short

Because like the black widow's bite

Her passion is like the venom

Her passion numbs your senses

Letting her consume you

And as you look into her eyes

You see only her love for you

All the while she feasts on your mind

Taking also your heart, body , and soul

She is so careful, so gentle as she feeds

Softly making love to you

While your heartbeat slows
You still smile at her

Unaware that you are slowly ceasing to exist
You hold on a little longer
Eager for her to climax
Taking you to heights you have never seen
And that she does
Smothering you in her sweetness

Your last breath
You breathe her
Your last taste
You taste her
Carefully she lays you down
And as you slip into darkness
She wraps you lovingly
In passion's web

Morning comes
You waken,
Remembering, trembling
You look over

You see her face

You touch her

She wakes and smiles at you

She is happy

She has nothing but love in her eyes for you

She says, yes my love

It was only a dream

Our love is forever

We are one soul, one mind, one heart

For us, forever is not short

Somewhere, we've shared a past

Now we have the present

And somehow I know

We will continue to find each other

For all eternity.......

PLEASURE

It is quiet, she is alone
She turns on her bath water
It is warm, inviting
She finds her favorite scent
This is pleasure

The water, the perfect temperature
She removes her robe
She watches herself undress
She enjoys seeing herself
She knows this is a part of her sexuality

She lights her candles
Sliding her naked body into the water
Her skin tingles
Her body craving her own touch
She knows what pleases her

Soft caresses with her fingertips
She finds her special place

The water consumes her
She is alone
She closes her eyes

She enjoys her soft touch
Knowing her body so well
Knowing what her body craves
With every touch she feels warmer
With every caress, her body craves more

She feels her orgasm building
Sweat now beads on her brow
She clenches her teeth
Her body releases
She explodes in ecstasy
She holds her breath
Letting herself go
Slowly she calms
Her breathing slows
She smiles, so relaxed

She feels pleasure
She knows her own sensuality

She knows her special place
The place that gives her pleasure
She is alone

The warmth of the water
The softness of her own touch
The scent of the oils
Touching all of her senses
She smiles

She is relaxed
But she wonders
How did she find this place
Why does her body crave this time
She is alone

She knows she craves comfort
She craves the warmth
She craves the soft caress
When all is quiet
She craves this place

She needs the comfort

She needs the warmth

She needs the soft caress

She has come to need this place

She is alone

She is her only comfort

She is her only friend

She is her only lover

She is saddened by this thought

Suddenly

The water turns cold

A WOMAN'S THOUGHTS:
INFIDELITY

Time alone , and her thoughts run free
She sees herself in the arms of another
For a brief time, her heart is set aside
Her sensuality awakens, raw passion set free
They explore each other with touch
No words are spoken, no words are needed
Her fingers slowly find his areas of pleasure
Slipping slowly down his back
Her mouth tasting the sweetness of his lips
His arms holding her tighter
He lays her gently on his pillow
Kissing her deeply, pausing for one moment
Softly licking and sucking her lips
Surprised for a second, yet she trembles
She is lost in her hunger for him
Her body is so warm now, she smiles
She feels his heat also, he looks into her eyes
She also feels his hardness against her
Her hunger grows, she is so wet now

She arches her body beneath him

Wanting to feel him inside her

He whispers in her ear........

Not yet love

His voice so soft, she melts.............

Let me taste you

She feels his mouth now nibble her ear

She closes her eyes as his lips go down her neck

His tongue licking down her chest

Licking and sucking each nipple with equal care

She is his now, no turning back

Nor does she want to

She is where she wants to be

She feels his tongue go further down

He now makes tiny circles around her navel

It is like a hidden pass key

Signaling her thighs to open

He now snuggles deep into her wetness

Taking in the sweet scent of her sensuality

She anticipates the feel of his tongue

Her body tenses

She holds her breath

Then she feels him

His tongue feasting on her very essence

She lets go, her orgasm feeding his hunger

He can hold no longer

He places his body over her

Slowly he slides deep inside her

She wraps her arms around him

He pulls her closer

Their bodies melt together

Their temperatures rise

They move together like a slow dance

Exotic, erotic, while the only music heard

Plays in their mind

Suddenly they climax together

At the same moment, she hears a sound

Quickly, coming back to reality

She turns the water off

As her sink runs over

DESIRE

She has a need
It leaves her restless
It haunts her sleep
It is but one need
She knows it so well
It's name is desire
She holds desire close
It is part of her

Desire
A soft touch
It awakens her body
A gentle kiss
It breathes life into her soul
A tender caress
Leaving her wanting more

Desire
Bodies melting in pleasure
Becoming as one

Erasing the outside world

Lost in each others touch

So sensual this moment

Creating such a force

Envied by nature itself

Desire

Climaxing together

Knowing each other's thoughts

Thoughts of pure passion

Searched for by many

Found by so few

They have found ecstasy

Desire

She knows this need

She holds it, she feels it

She breathes it

She is..

Desire

A PRECIOUS GIFT

He comes to her

He smiles

His eyes so dark

They look so warm

He touches her gently

She feels so content

He loves her

She sees it in his eyes

She feels it in his touch

This is where she belongs

In his arms

It feels right

It must be right

He gave her a gift

A gift she holds close

It is forever hers

He gave her his heart

She holds it close

He kisses her

She feels complete

She feels whole again

She returns the kiss

And to him also, a gift

She gives to him her heart

He holds her close

Their bodies become one

Making love until dawn

Making their worlds complete

And to each other

They promise their hearts

Forever until death

And, after their last breath

Throughout eternity

WHISPERS

A feeling comes over her

She feels a soft breeze

She smiles

She hears the soft voice

It whispers

Suddenly, she feels so warm

No more coldness in her heart

She is happy

She finally hears the sounds

She hears the whispers

It is him

She hears his voice, so soft

So loving is the sound

It is real

She can feel it, so warm

She sleeps , happy now

She feels comfort

Her mind will rest freely

She hears him and smiles

As he whispers

I love you

Passion's love of family

Being raised by a strong, loving family still happens, and Passion was one of the lucky ones to be blessed with this type of family.

A father who worked hard and a mother that was the giver and the caretaker of all of us. Passion has a family of her own now, and strives to bring the same giving and caretaking to her family that she saw as she grew. The following tells a little of how she feels for all of them............

I Love You All Deeply

THE MEANING OF LOVE

Look into a child's eyes
The sincere love in those eyes for momma
When they fall, momma can fix it
When they get dirty, momma can clean them
When they are sad, only momma's hug soothes them
When they are mad, only momma can calm them
While they grow, the values they carry begin with momma
As adults, they pray that momma is proud
She is not only momma, she is a best friend
When a momma is lost, you still strive to please her
You want her to look down from heaven, and still be proud
People look a lifetime for the true meaning of love
All they have to do, is look into a child's eyes
As they look and smile at their momma
They soon realize, where to find the true
Meaning of love

A LETTER TO YOU

First of all, I love you
You are the rock I lean on
I may not say it enough
And sometimes
I'm too far away to show it
But you made me who I am
Sometimes, we tend to forget
Momma washes our little faces
Momma cooks the food we eat
But you worked hard for us
Your long hours
Brought food to the kitchen
Your long hours
Kept clothes on our backs
Momma gave us discipline, but
Avoiding the disappointment in your eyes
Kept us in line more
Now a momma with my own family
Watching my husband do as you did
I know deep in my heart

I was dearly loved

And you gave us your all

Daddy, you mean the world to me

ADMIRATION FOR ALL THAT YOU ARE

Over the years you have been
So many different women in my life
As a student in school, you were a role model
As a wife, you taught me important values
Giving me the keys to a lasting relationship
As a mother, you have raised a lady
She is as precious as pure crystal
As well as strong as steel
I have watched you go down
Almost giving up
I have watched you pick yourself up
Standing proud and dusting yourself off
My heart warms, just thinking of your strength
Thinking of all the things you are to me
I admire every part of what makes you my sister
Your strength when you are weak
Your smiles when you are in pain
Your laughter when you feel like crying
But most of all
I am proud to call you
My big sister

For my big sister with my love

SISTERS

As children, we fought and played
We laughed at the silliest things
We cried, sometimes over nothing
When threatened, we protected each other

Now, we are women no longer playing
We still laugh, we still cry
Our bond is still strong
Now as women, we long for that childhood
If only for a moment
For we have seen each other through so many things
Death
Divorce
Sickness
And many times, our bond is tested
But still it holds strong

From a distance, we still hold hands
From a distance, we hold each other as we cry
From a distance, the love is still shared

From a distance, we hear each other's prayer

We say a prayer for our sister
A prayer for long life
A prayer for happiness
A prayer for strength
A prayer for hope

There is no love like that of a sister
No bond goes deeper, no ties stronger

Say a prayer, and give love to our sister
God is listening, and he will help us be strong

For my sisters
With all my love

A REFLECTION OF SHE

As a small child, she played in the sun
She smiled and was happy about the little things
The movement of clouds amazed her mind
The thought of god up there
Watching her, hiding behind the clouds
She asked so many questions
Sometimes, even understanding the answers
Happy to absorb the world around her
Growing in size and knowledge
It was like an adventure to her
So, with the help of that watching god
And parents who taught her well
She grew to be a woman
A wife, a mother, happy and proud
But, sometimes missing that small child
The light in those eyes
The questions on that small mind
Brings the occasional tear to her eyes
But when she misses that child she was
She looks down

Smiles, and suddenly her heart warms
She is looking into the eyes of her own child
And in her daughter's eyes
There is a clear reflection
Reflections of the child that once was she

WHAT YOU MEAN TO ME

Loving you has been a joy in my life
All the things you have done for me meant so much
Times we talked, times we have cried
Opening your heart and letting me in
You have grown to be a woman now
A strong female with a strong mind
All the things you have become have made me so proud
No young lady I have ever known compares to you
It will be hard to let go, but I am secure in knowing this...
Someday, others will be blessed by knowing you as I do
Each time I have that thought, it warms my heart and I
smile

For my oldest daughter,
I love you

ONCE IN A LIFETIME I FOUND THAT ONE LOVE

The one person that brings me to life
Each day of my lifetime, I thank god above
That I have that one love, and I am his wife

For my husband
I love you

THOUGHTS FOR MY HUSBAND

Growing in your love
The first kiss from you was like a seed planted
Your tender love was like caring for a growing tree
You have watched me go through so many changes
And with each change my heart grew bigger and stronger
Now, with your love I am strong and I have grown
With your presence, I am like spring blossoming to full
beauty
With your absence, I am like the fall, leaves dying, falling
away
My love for you is like the roots of this great tree
Growing deeper and stronger with each passing year
And I know in the future as time goes bye
Your place in my heart gets bigger, and my love for you
more dear

I love you

DEDICATION TO A TRUE FRIEND

I see in your eyes, a strength within
Unnoticed by some, concealed by gentleness
I hear in your laugh, a strength
Sure of who and what you are

I feel myself feeding off your strength
In times of need
Longing for the sound of your laugh
Finding a light in those eyes
When I am in darkness

Your inner strength is your power
Yet you have never discovered it
It stays well hidden
You will find later in life
The strength I see in you
But only as a reflection
It will be in the eyes of your children
As they look up to you

A THANK YOU NOTE

To the reader

I hope you found something in my thoughts and my words that you may have enjoyed or maybe even touched you in some slight way. Thank you for your time and attention and for purchasing my first work. There will be more and I hope you will be around for each and every piece I write. These poems are big part of myself that I love sharing with you. Again, thank you. Now, a few words for a couple of special people that have been with me since the very day I decided that it was time to share my thoughts.

Adrian

Yes, you really are like a son to me and I thank you for your calming words and support through those long nights when the tears flowed along with the poems. The times when three in the morning would still find you trying to get Passion to go to bed knowing you had to get up for work.

You always stayed until you knew I would rest peacefully, sometimes even calling to make sure I had finished crying and you could hear me smile.

Someday, I want you to finish the story about Lil Red In The Hood Okay?

Love you, Sho.

Tim

My Rock, what can I possibly say to you? You have been right there for every moment that I was excited about finishing a new piece or even crying frantically because the thoughts were there and the words just wouldn't come. You even had the guts and the strength to get behind me and push when you knew that it was just fear that blocked those words. You helped make me realize that I could no longer hold back and that I had to share this gift I was given. You also could tell when I needed my space and had to have time to myself so I could clear my head. I think you come close to reading my mind at times. All I can tell you is that without you I know that I would have stopped a year ago. Not my writing of course, but I would have put it back in the drawer and given up. You, in my heart are my brother and a very dear friend. Thank you for everything.

Love ya, AKIL.

Donnie

Last, but absolutely not least. You have known me for so many years and you have lived with the mind, body, and soul behind these words. You mean the world to me because I love you and because you loved me enough to give me the space emotionally that I needed to do this book. Sometimes I think I wanted to hear you say 'Baby don't do it, no one will read it' because I think that sometimes I was just afraid enough that I wanted a reason to quit, but not really say those words. I wanted to feel like I quit because you needed me to. But you believed in me and you held me up and reminded me at every turn that I could do this and that you would be there for me. As long as I have you, I am never alone. All I have to say to you is this, after all the years that we have been together, good times and bad, I still wake up everyday smiling and feeling proud that I am your wife.

I love you, Baby. You are forever my heart.

About the Author

I was born in a small town in Tennessee on December 5, 1962. The middle child in a family with five kids, I was a bit of a free thinker but at the same time, as normal as most children. My parents, (both still living and I thank God every day for that) raised us very well and gave us the love and discipline that we needed to become strong, family-oriented adults.

As a young girl, I found writing to be an outlet for me. Being a middle child is not that easy, I wasn't much for crying on anyone's shoulder and I was always a bit of a loner; therefore, I wrote my feelings much better than expressing them vocally. If my memory serves me correctly, I think I started writing poems around age 14. My favorite poet at that time was Edgar Allen Poe, only because his work was the first poetry that I actually felt. You could see his pain in his words and to me the writer as well as the reader should feel poetry.

Now at the age of 36, married 17 years to a wonderful man that loves and supports me 100% and two daughters of my own, I write most of the time for my own pleasure and relaxation. The content has changed in many ways from when I was a child, but the basis of my work remains the same. I write what I live, feel, and see.